ILLUSTRATED BIOGRAPHY FOR KIDS
NIKOLA TESLA
EXTRAORDINARY SCIENTIST
WHO CHANGED THE WORLD

Wonder House

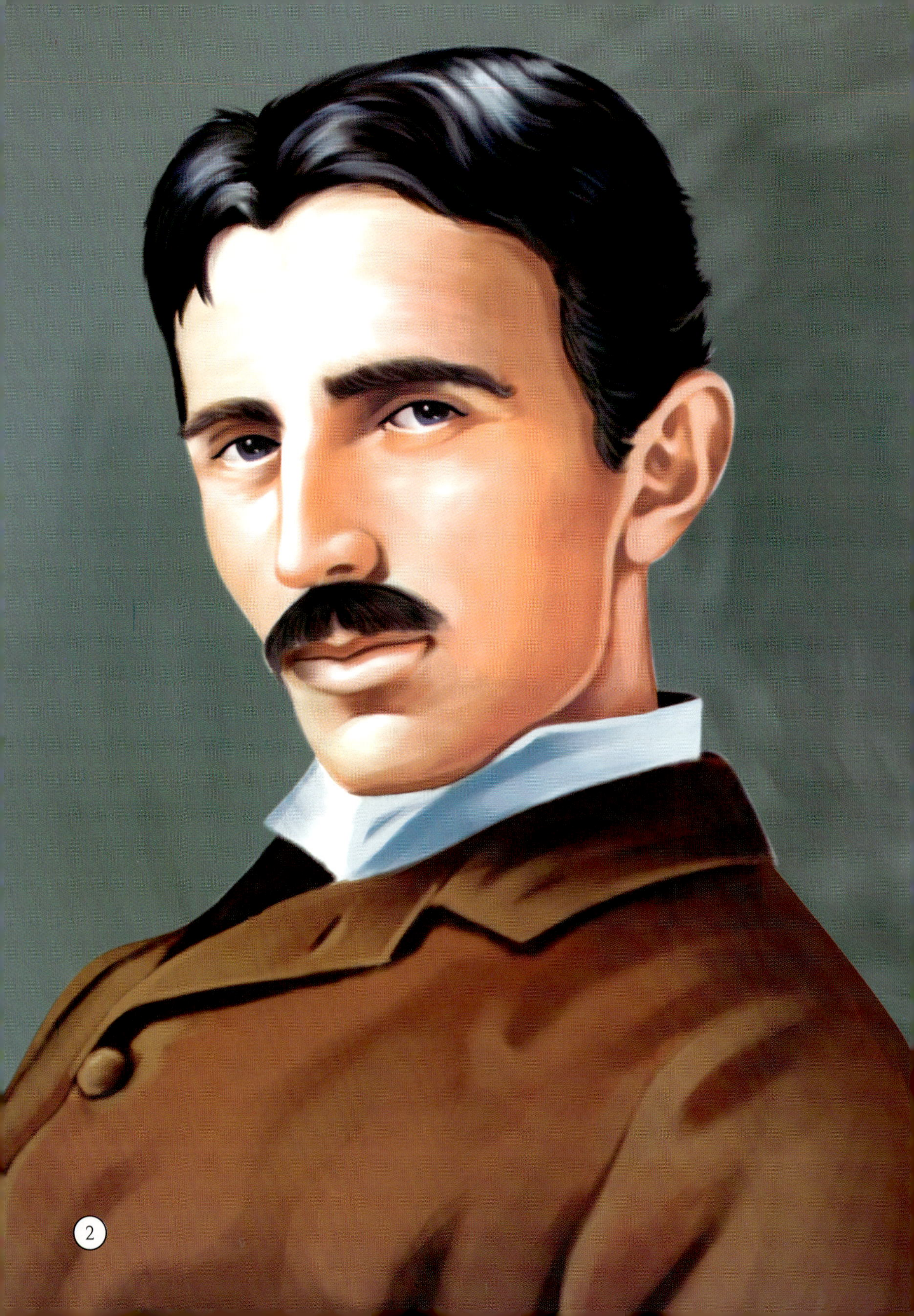

A MAN OF LOFTY GENIUS

Nikola Tesla was a prominent physicist, inventor, scientist, thinker and engineer of all time. Many of the inventions which are a part of our life today such as smartphones and wireless communication, were first proposed by him. He was a man of vision and unique insight who brought a revolution in the field of sciences; especially in the field of electrical engineering. He is best known for his invention of rotating magnetic field based on alternating current (AC).

In 1891, Tesla invented Tesla coil, and patented more than 300 inventions under his name. This brought him a lot of scientific acclaim for his discovery but still the road to success never ran straight for him. His ideas were far ahead of his time and often came in his way of success. As a man of strong ideals, he wanted to change the future of telecommunication and power transmission, and aspired to make the life of common people easy.

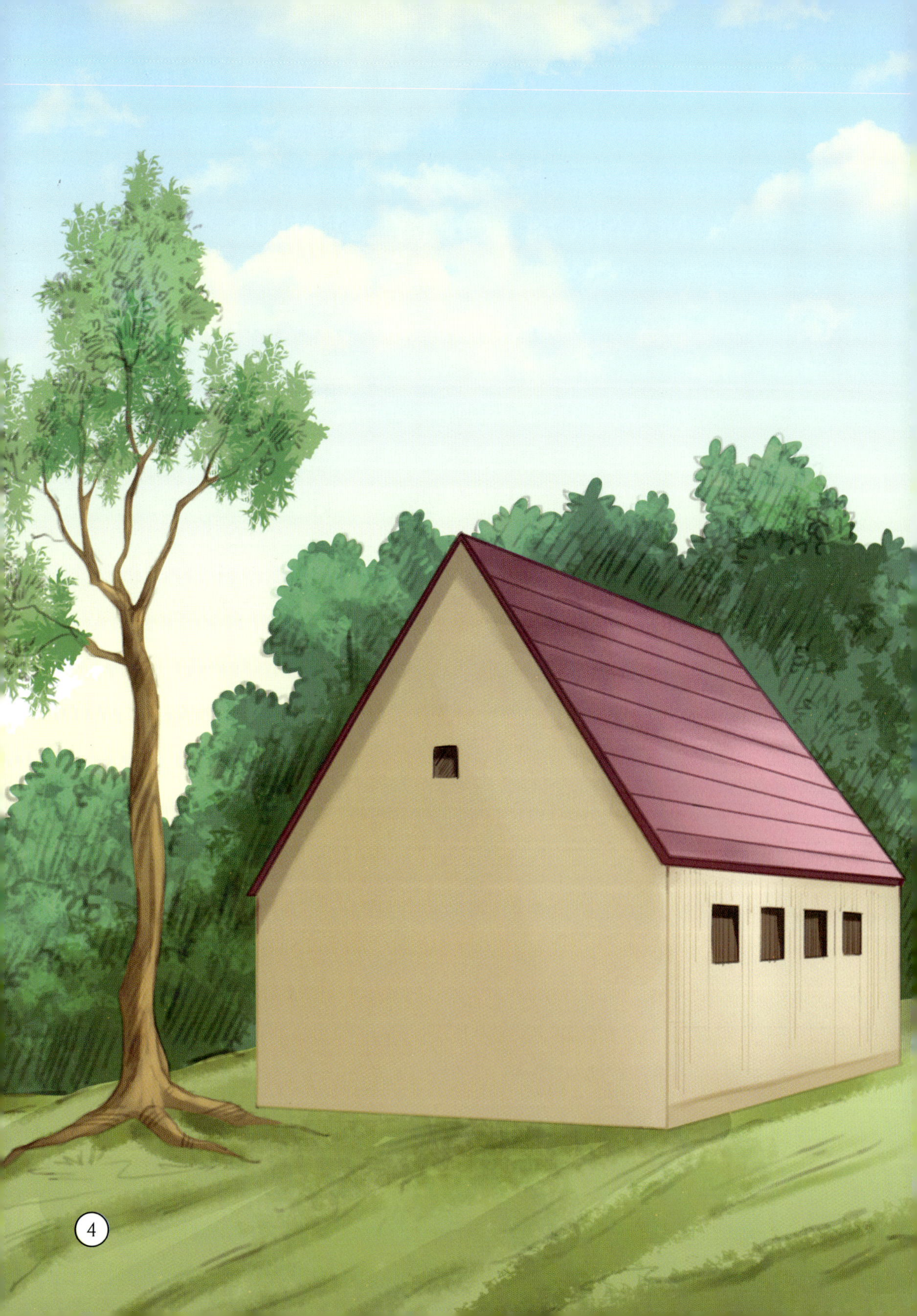

A GENIUS IS BORN

Nikola Tesla was born in modern-day Croatia in 1856. He was the fourth child born to his parents, his father was a priest and his mother was a homemaker. He learned a great deal from his mother; she possessed the talent of making and repairing mechanical appliances, and had a great liking for Serbian poetry which she had learned from heart. His mother's creative abilities had a very positive influence on Tesla. He learned from her and took after her, which also hints at his own liking towards poetry and resourcefulness in inventing things from scratch.

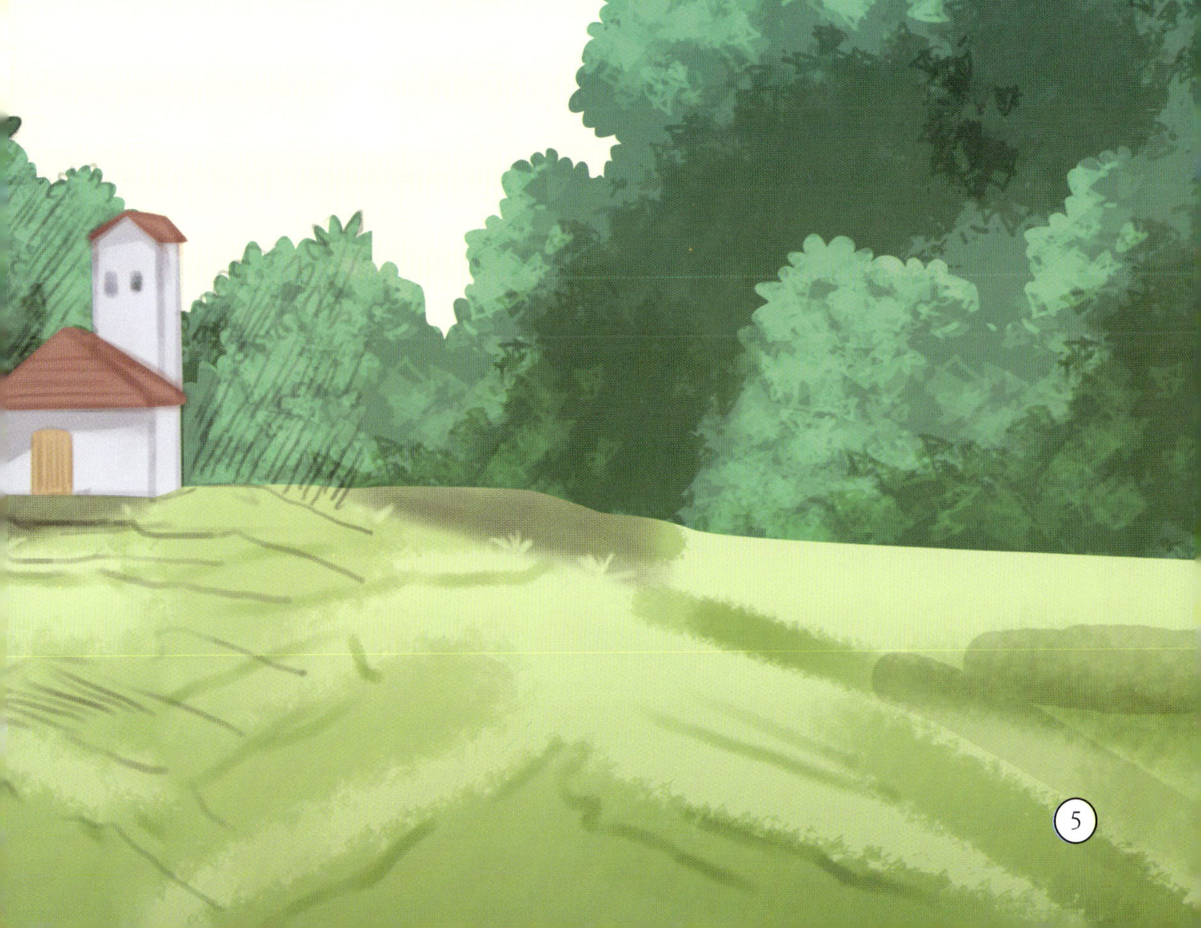

IT IS ALL IN THE HEAD

During his school days, Tesla had a huge inclination towards physics. He was amazed by the demonstrations of electricity in his physics class: this new force sparked such interest in him that he wanted to learn more about this mysterious phenomenon. He was an exceptional student and a fast learner; his studies were not only limited to the field of sciences but also ranged from poetry

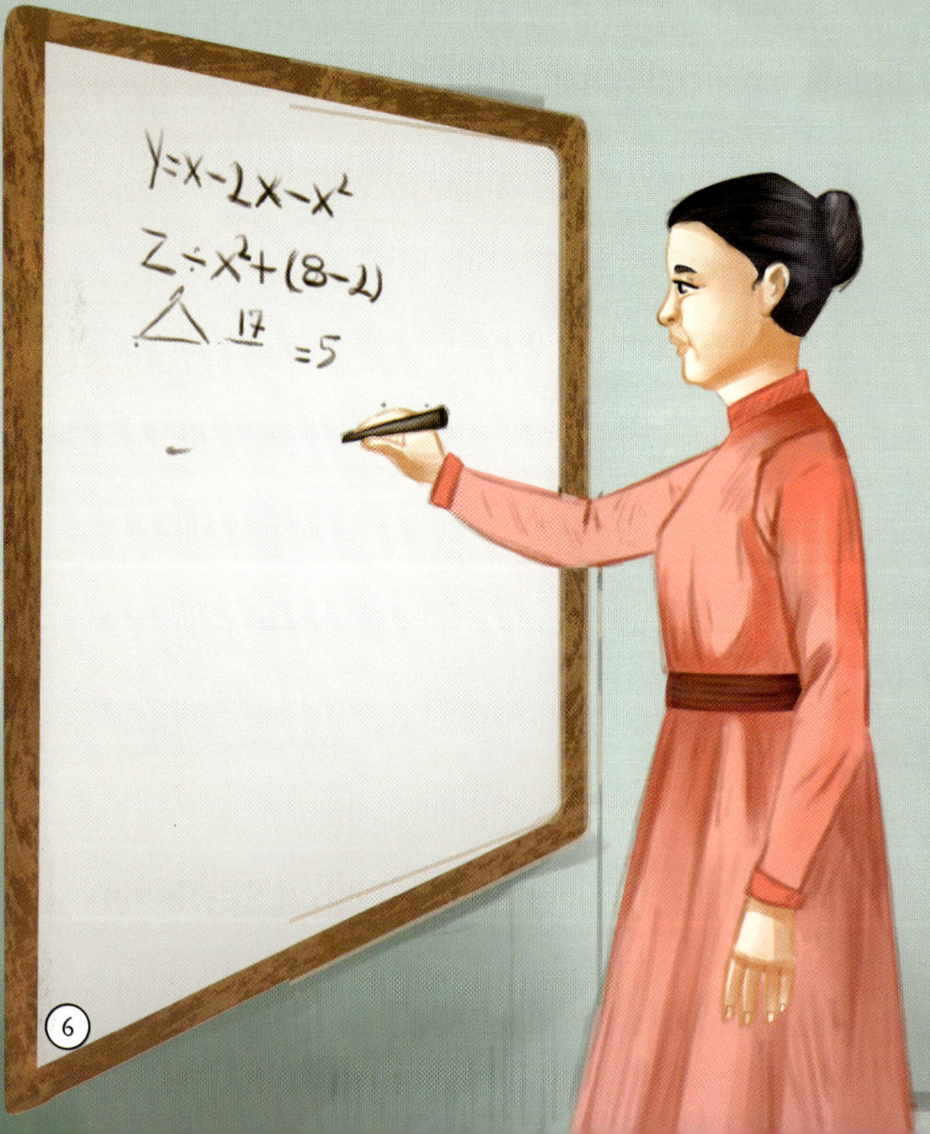
Y=X-2X-X²
Z÷X²+(8-2)
17
=5

to learning different languages. He was quick in understanding and recalling everything as it is and his eidetic memory amazed his teachers so much that they doubted whether he was cheating on his tests. At a very young age, he could memorize the books and recite the logarithmic tables as it is. He was so good with calculations that even before the teacher could finish the question on board, he would be ready with the answers.

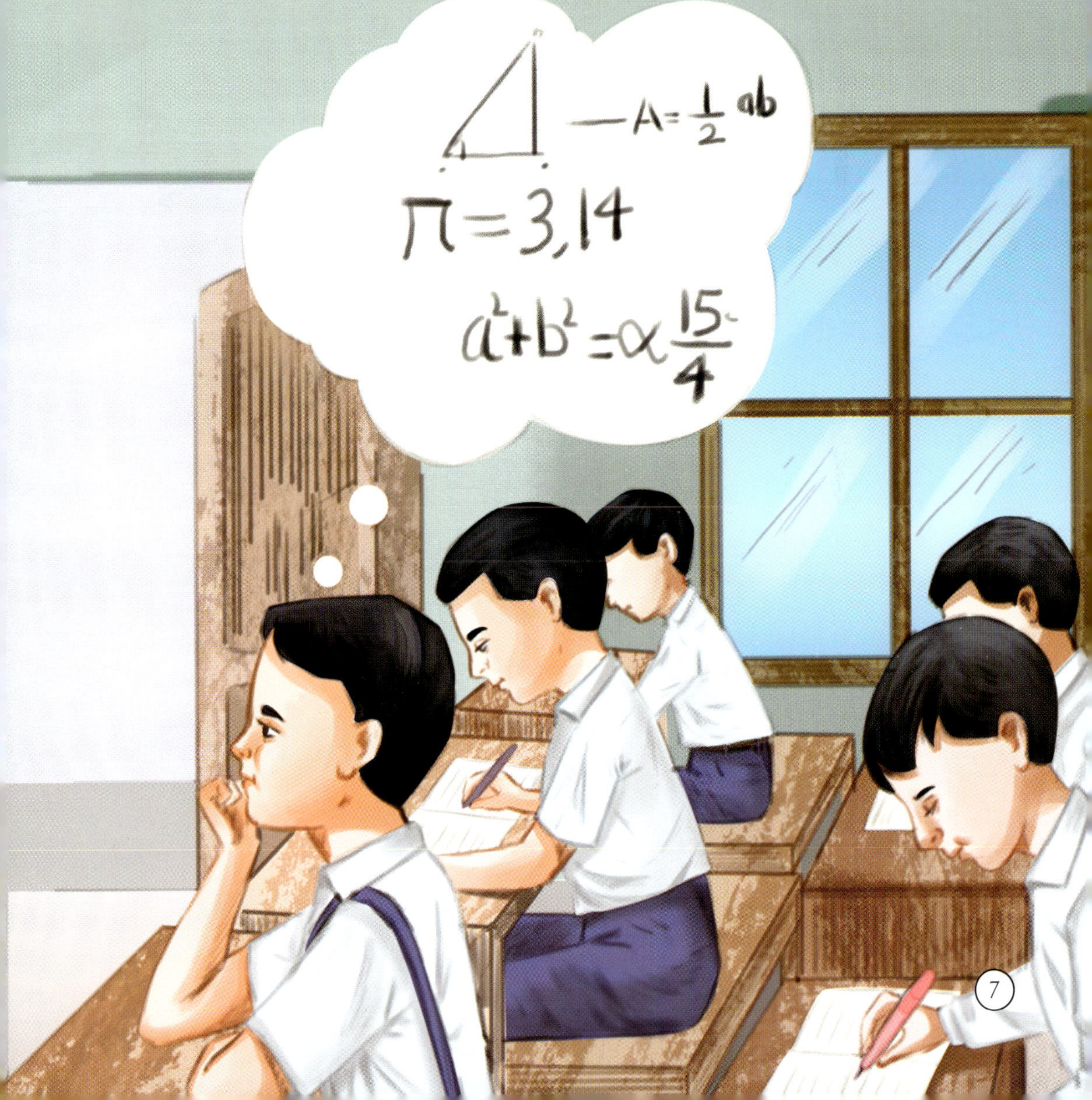

A= 1/2 ab
π=3,14
a²+b² =α 15/4

ROAD TO WILDERNESS

In 1875, at the age of 19, Tesla enrolled in the Imperial-Royal Technical College in Graz, Austria. As soon as he joined the college, he was proclaimed the star student; he proved his intelligence and natural genius by pointing out the design flaws in the direct-current (DC) motors that were being demonstrated during one of the classes. He made suggestions for the improvement of its design that amazed his professor.

For the first two years in college, he excelled brilliantly in his studies, but by the third year, he was failing in all the subjects. It has been said, during this time he was addicted to gambling and lost all his tuition fees and soon he dropped out of the college. After this event, Tesla suffered a major nervous breakdown.

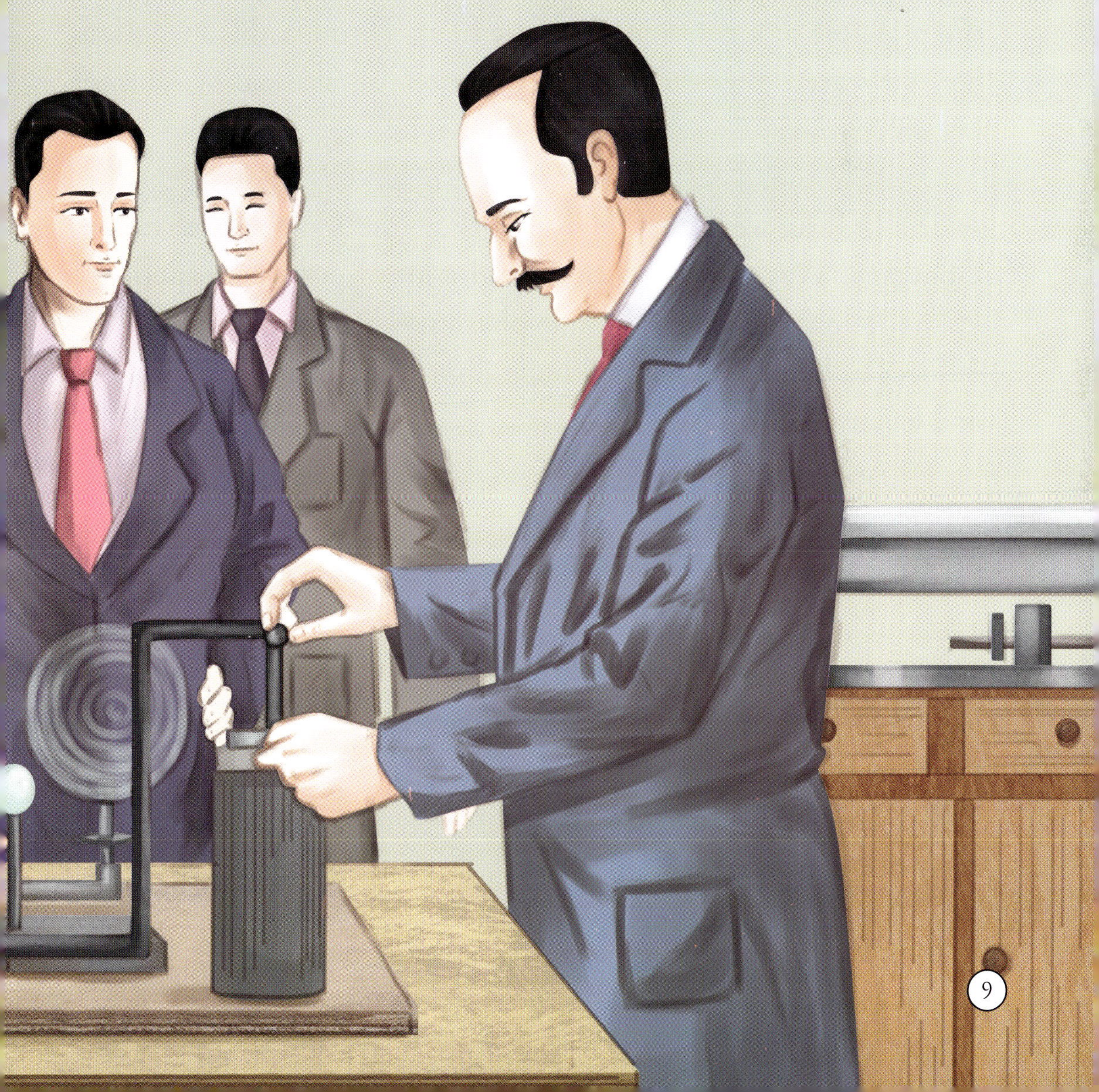

WITH NEW BEGINNINGS COME NEW LEARNINGS

In 1881, after recovering from his breakdown, Tesla moved to Budapest to work at the Budapest Telephone Exchange as a chief electrician. During this time, while strolling in the park with a friend, he came up with the idea of an induction motor based on the principle of a rotating magnetic field. Through this invention, he showcased the successful utilization of alternating current (AC).

In 1882, Tesla went to Paris to work at the Continental Edison Company. Working there, he gained a lot of practical experience in the field of engineering and physics. This experience further influenced him to design and build improved versions of dynamos and electric motors.

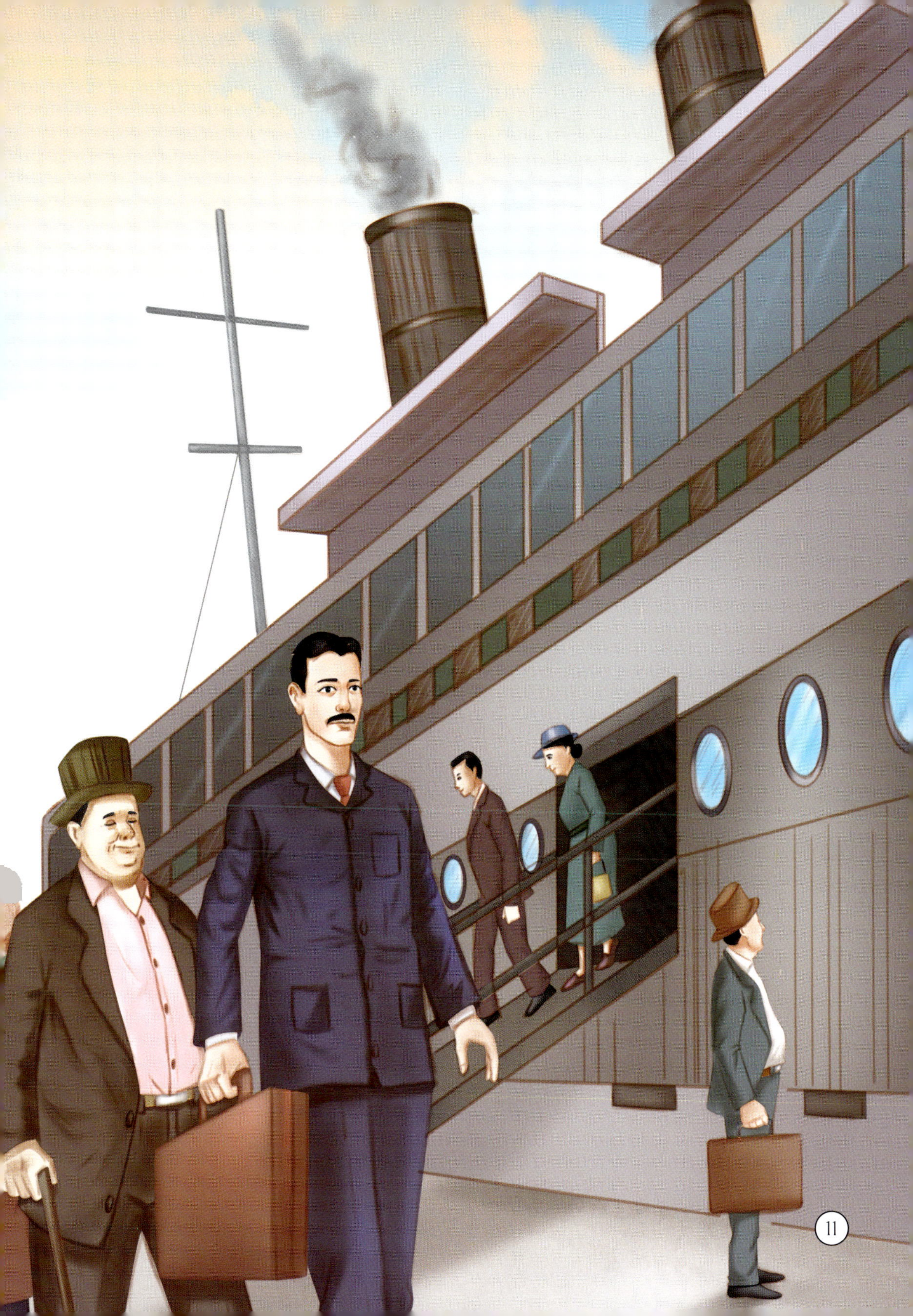

In 1884, he moved to New York City with only four cents and a letter of recommendation addressed to Thomas Edison, by his former employer, Charles Batchelor.

Tesla worked at Edison's factory for only a few months and left the facility soon. He improved the working of Edison utilities and helped in redesigning of DC generators. Though it is not clearly known why and how Tesla and Edison fell apart but some claim that—it was because of Edison's refusal to pay Tesla the stipulated amount which he promised to him for redesigning the DC generators.

This event had a significant impact on their relation, which severed more in the later years. Some thinkers have claimed that both Tesla and Edison were very different from each other in terms of their methods and approach, so it came as no surprise that the two men who were poles apart from each other fell out so soon.

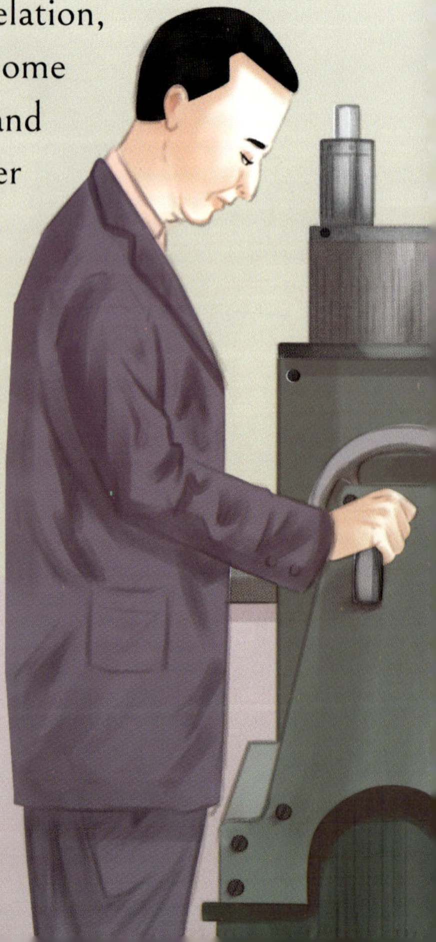

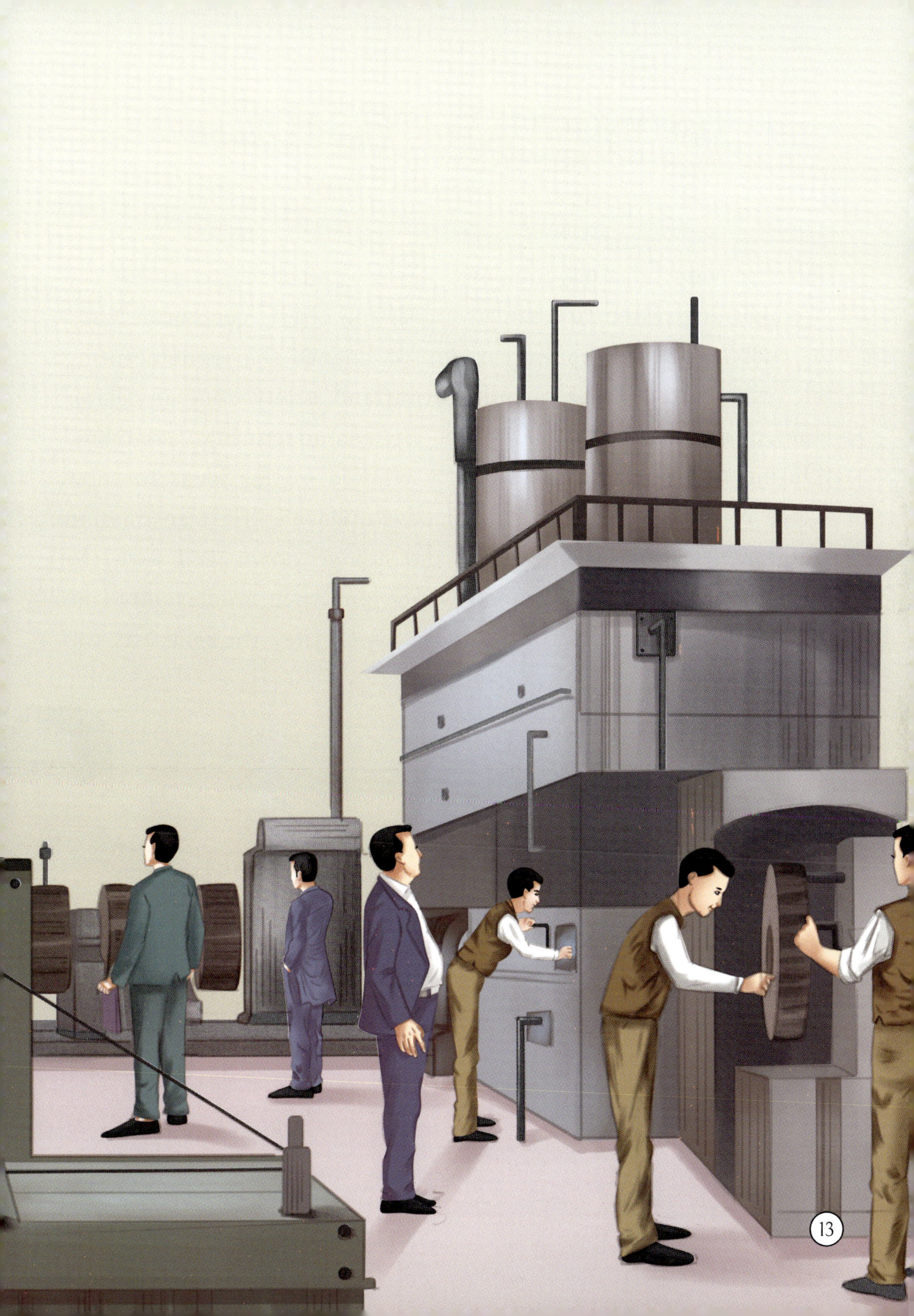

TESTING THE WATERS FOR THE FIRST TIME

After leaving Edison's company, Tesla went ahead to patent the arc lightning system and improved version of DC generator. Soon he met investors who were ready to finance the manufacturing of Tesla's arc lighting manufacturing and utility company, later named as, Tesla Electric Light & Manufacturing Company. During this time, Tesla diligently worked on his ideas for new types of alternating current and developed electric transmission equipments. But his new ideas did not go down well with the investors who were apprehensive to put their money into the manufacturing side of the business which they thought was too competitive.

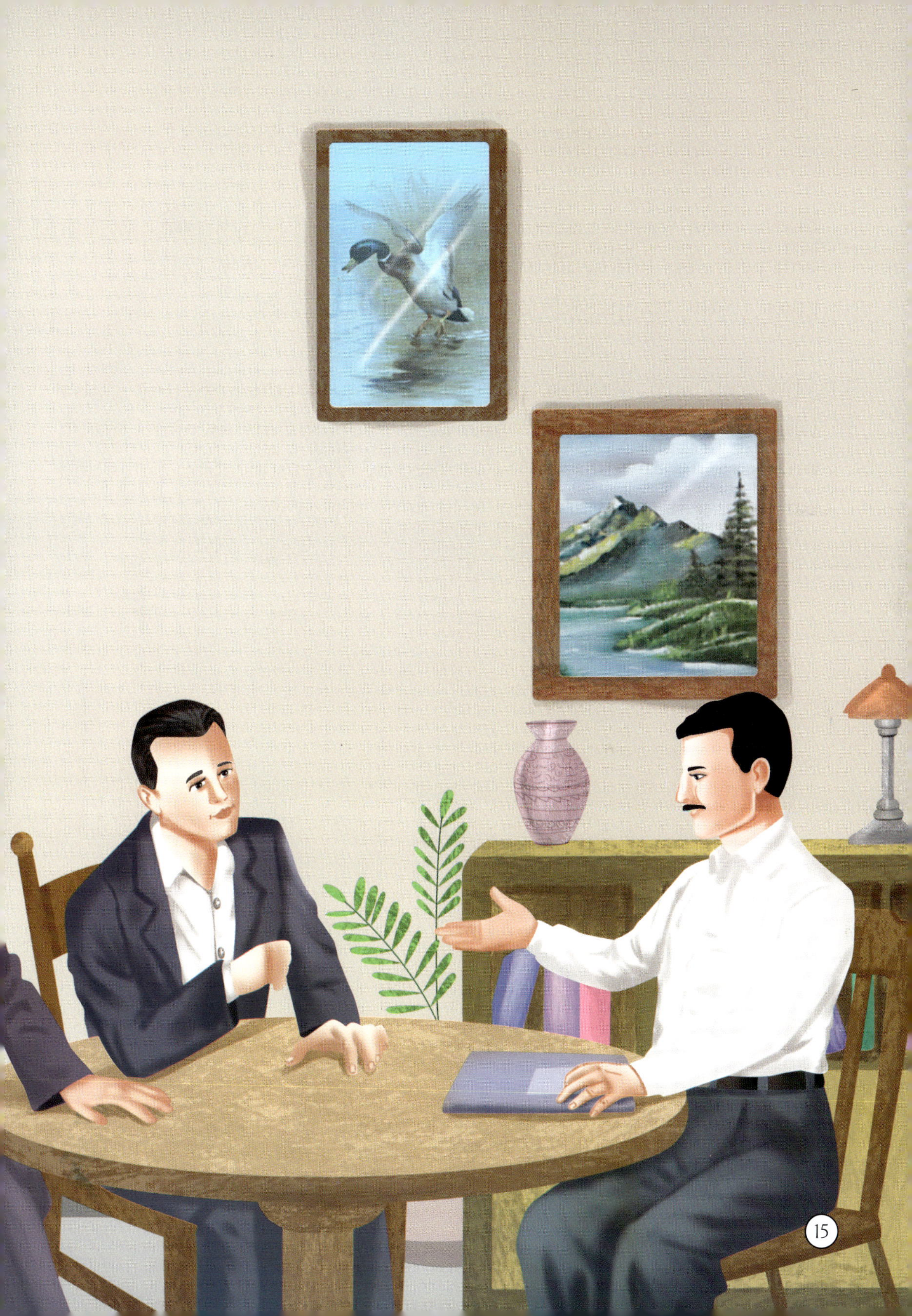

QUESTIONING LIFE

Soon Tesla was abandoned by his investors, which not only left him penniless but he also lost control of his patents which he had given to the company in exchange for the stocks.

This was particularly a very tough time for the inventor. After being abandoned by his investors, He took to menial jobs in order to sustain himself. He worked at various electrical jobs and earned his living by working as a ditch digger earning $2 per day.

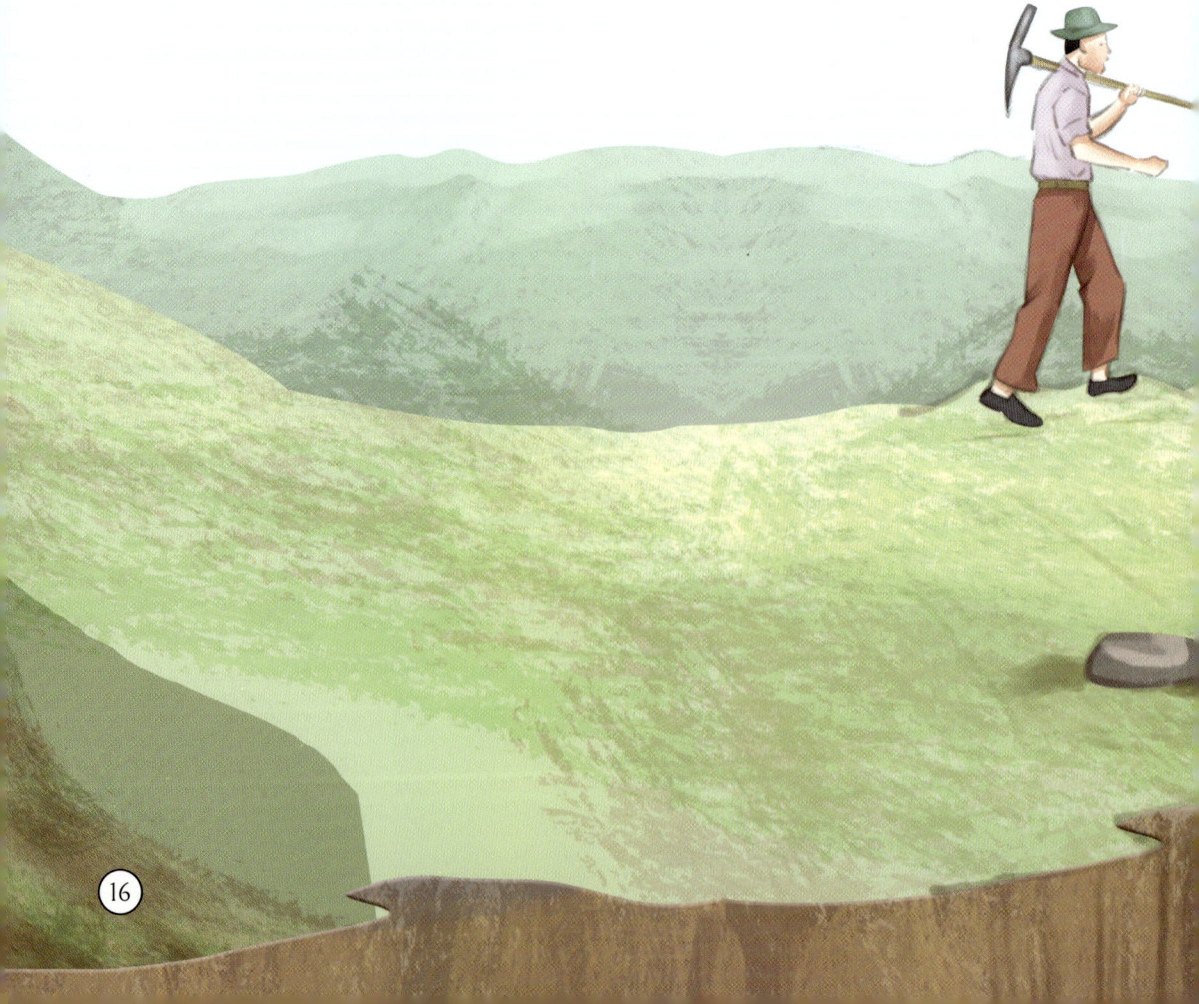

He questioned his life ambitions and education in the field of sciences and engineering. At this time his life-long education and discoveries seemed like a mockery to him!

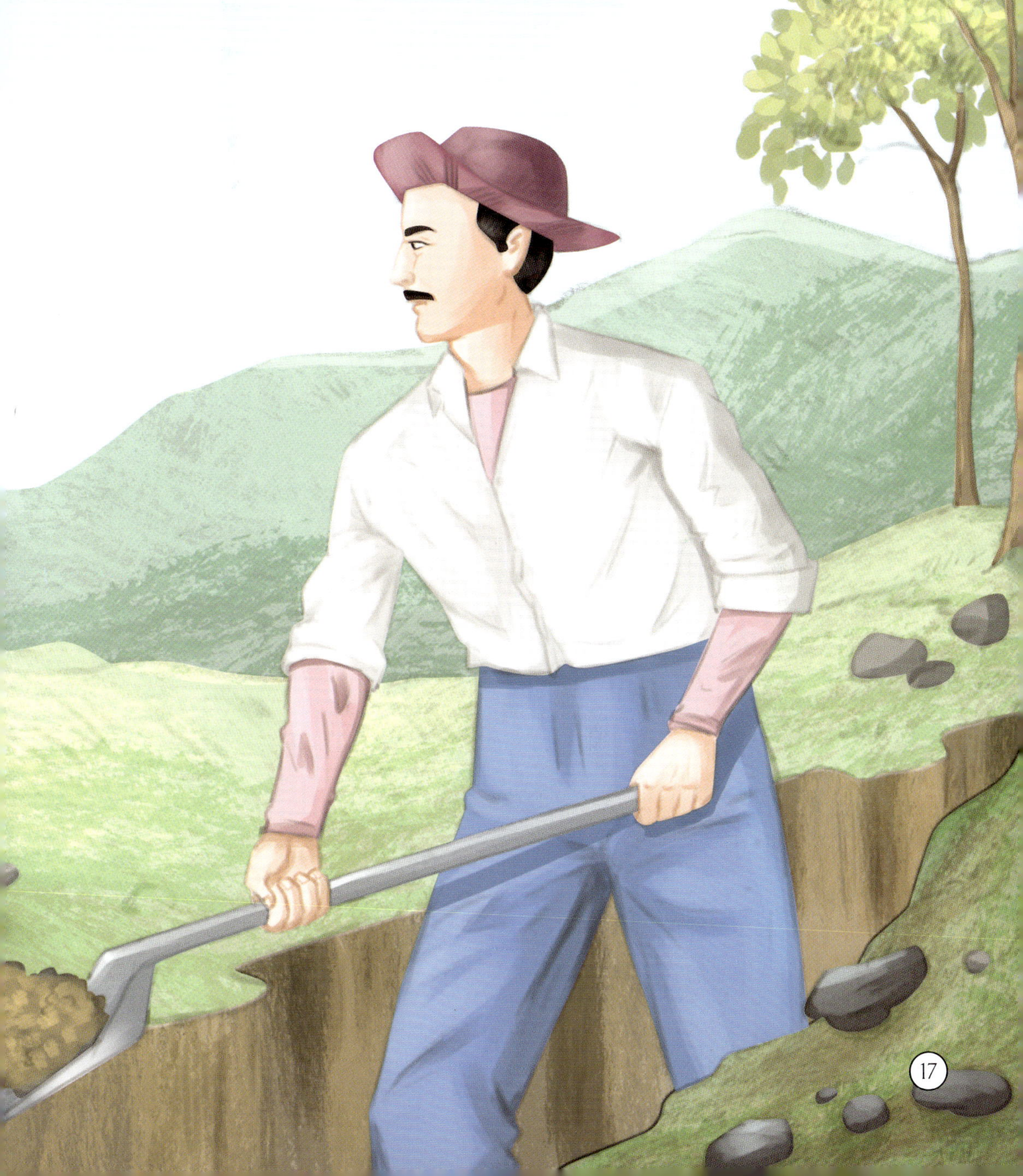

EVERY CLOUD HAS A SILVER LINING

In 1887, Tesla with the help of two businessmen, Alfred S. Brown and Charles Fletcher Peck established the Tesla Electric Company, with an agreement to equally divide the profits. In this new facility, Tesla worked on improving the new types of electric motors, generators, and other devices.

He developed an induction motor based on alternating current (AC), a phenomenon that was rapidly gaining a lot of attention due to its advantages for long-distance transmission, high voltage, low maintenance and safety. His discovery was highly publicized and received a lot of media attention. This came to the attention of George Westinghouse, the owner of Westinghouse Electric and Manufacturing Company.

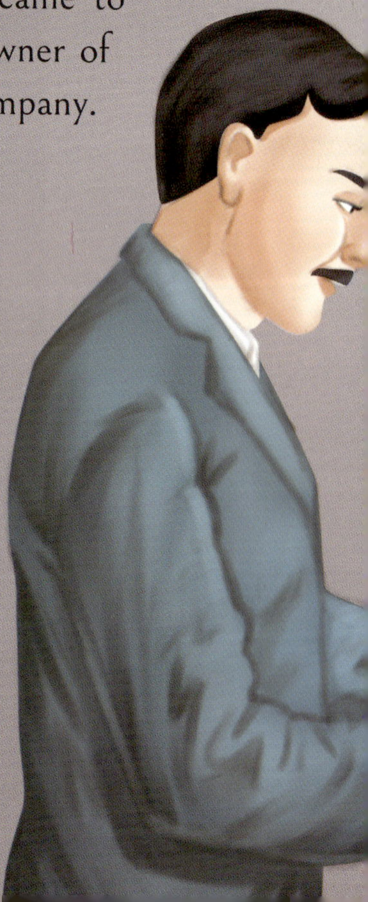

In 1888, Tesla signed a deal with Westinghouse for an Induction motor and transformer design, for $60,000 in cash and a royalty of $2.50 per AC horsepower produced by each motor. He was hired by the Westinghouse as a consultant for one year for a large fee of $2,000 per month.

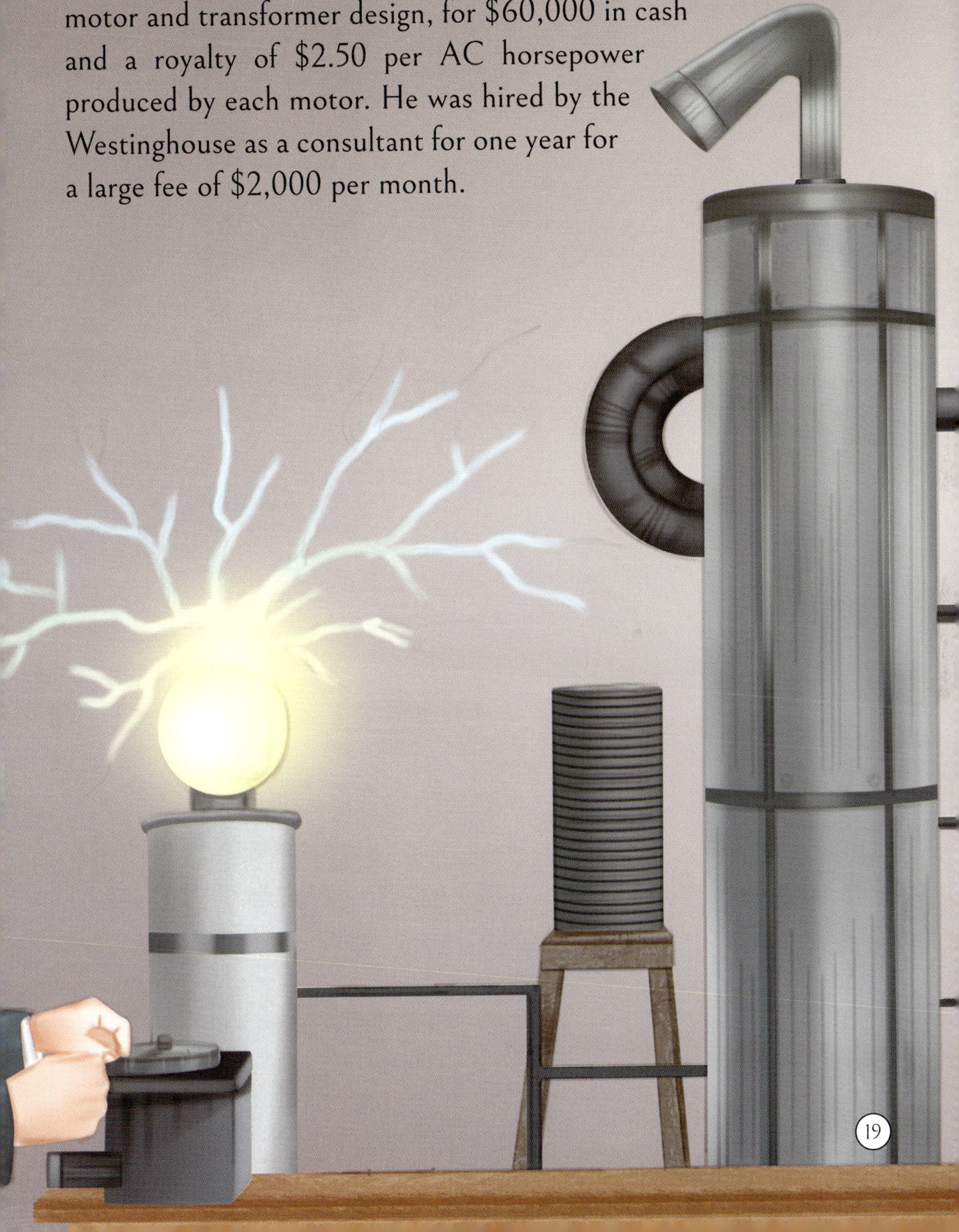

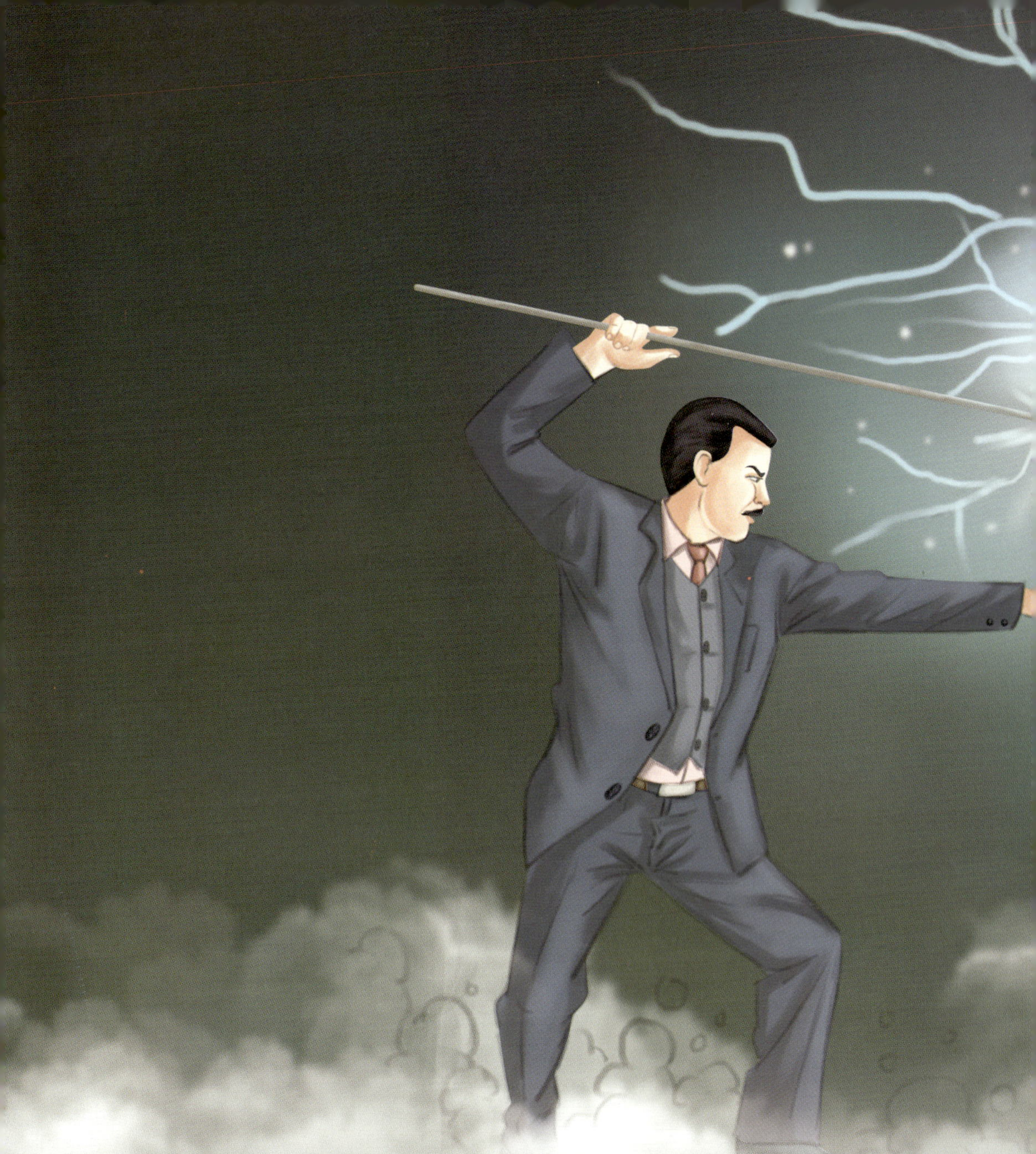

Tesla and Edison were embroiled in the 'War of Electric Currents', Edison and his supporters were of view that the direct current system was better than the alternating current. This war of currents was particularly difficult for Westinghouse who was backing Tesla and his alternating current systems. The high cost of fighting a legal

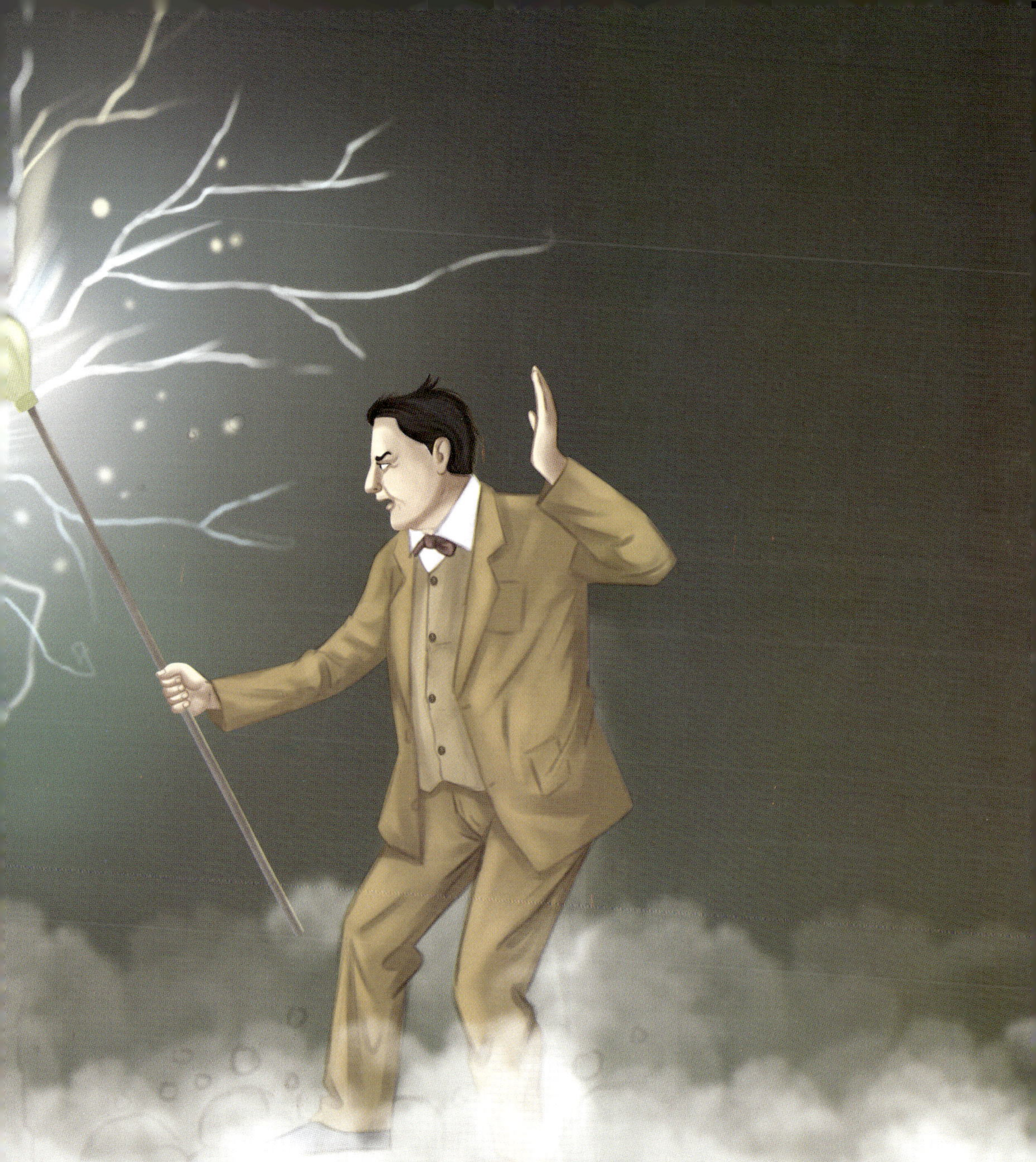

battle forced Westinghouse to ask Tesla for relief from paying him the royalties. Tesla, being grateful to Westinghouse relinquished the royalty papers. It has been claimed that, if Tesla had not taken this decision, then he would have been one of the wealthiest men in the world!

TESLA COILS

Around 1891, Tesla invented powerful coils called 'Tesla Coils'. These coils could generate high voltage frequencies, and made it possible to send and receive radio signals. Tesla quickly filed for their patents beating the Italian inventor Guglielmo Marconi. The Tesla coil has been widely used in radio and television sets and various other electronic equipments.

Meanwhile, in order to dispel the rumors surrounding the alternating current (AC), together Tesla and Westinghouse used the AC system to light the 1893 World's Columbian Exposition in Chicago. This successful show helped Westinghouse to bag the contract to install the first power station at Niagara Falls.

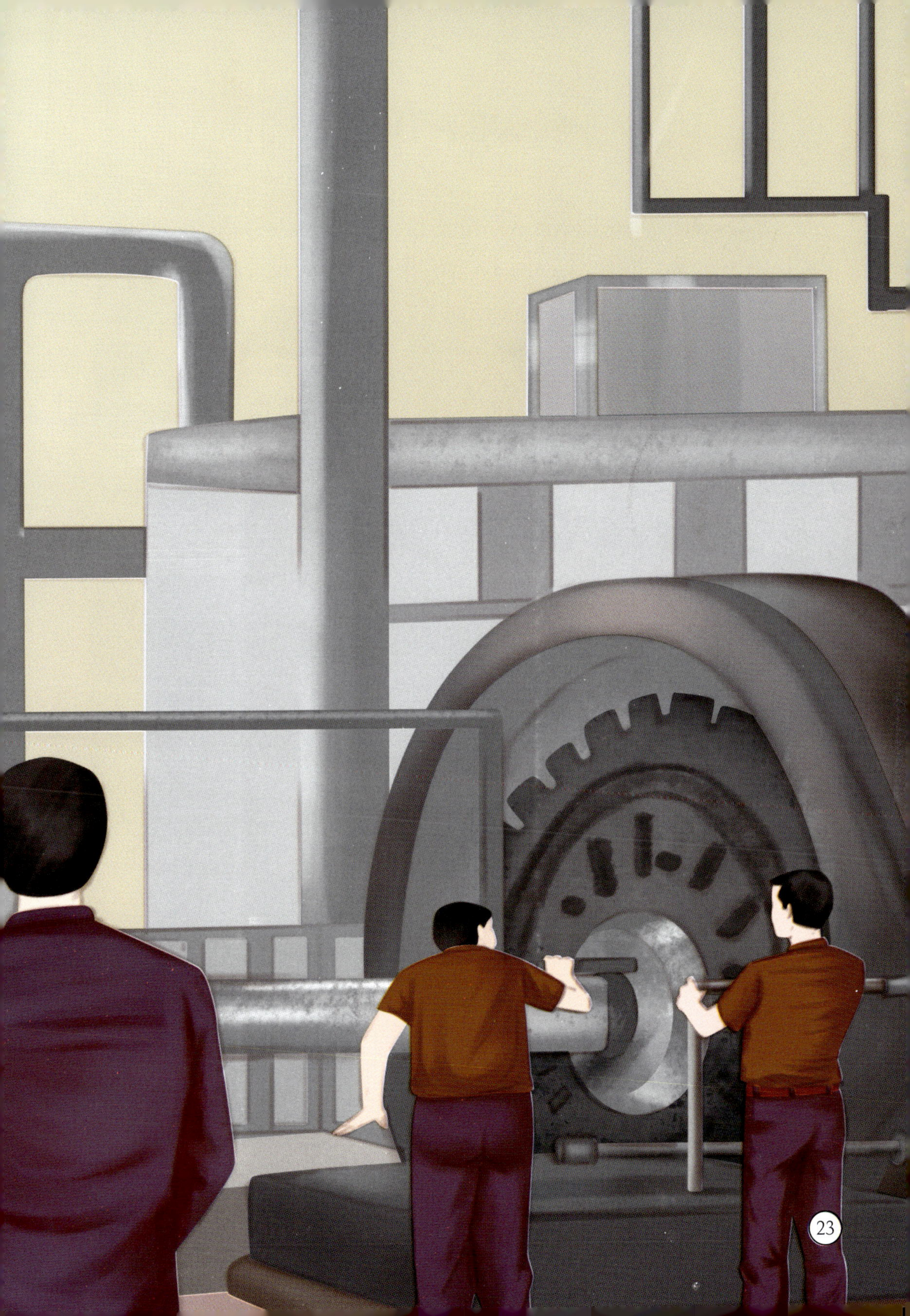

I HAVE A DREAM

Tesla gave the world many mind-blowing inventions that shaped it into what it is today. In 1898, Tesla demonstrated in a public

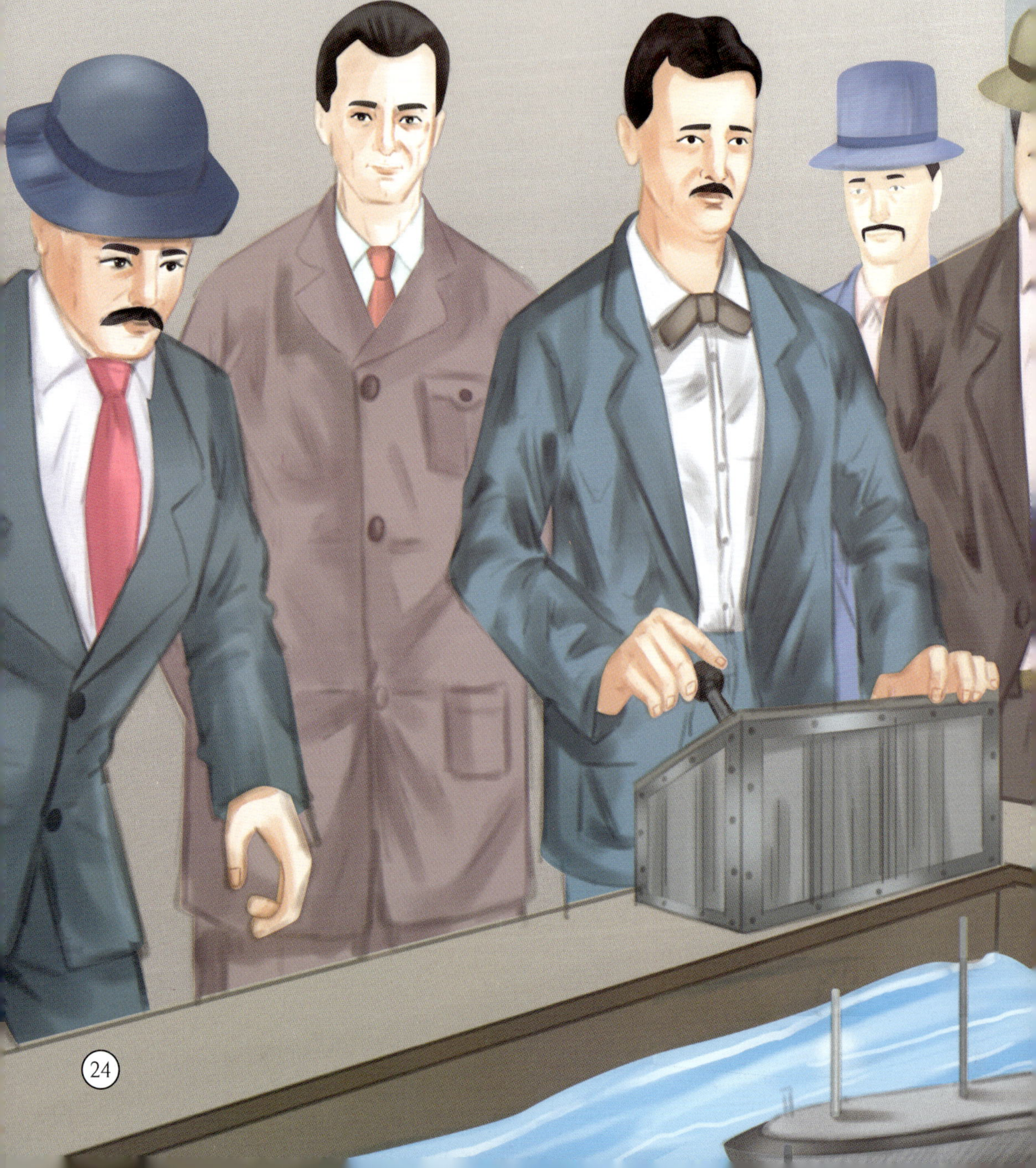

exhibition, the working of a radio-controlled automated boat. Later he spent most of his fortune on developing several projects based on wireless power, an idea through which he wanted to change the functioning of the world.

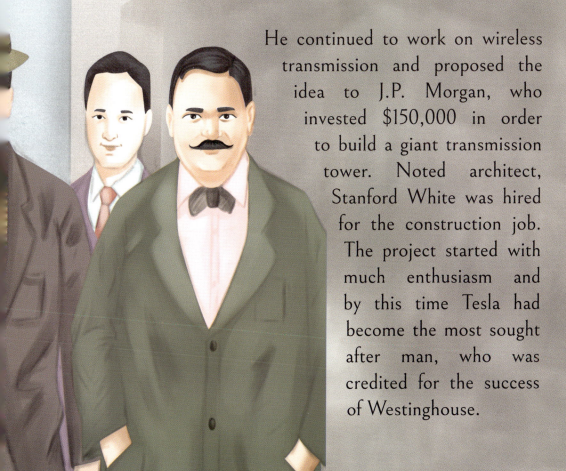

He continued to work on wireless transmission and proposed the idea to J.P. Morgan, who invested $150,000 in order to build a giant transmission tower. Noted architect, Stanford White was hired for the construction job. The project started with much enthusiasm and by this time Tesla had become the most sought after man, who was credited for the success of Westinghouse.

In 1901, White started his work of designing the Wardenclyffe Tower, but the money invested in the construction soon ran out. Morgan on the other hand refused to invest more money in the construction. Thus, the 186-foot-tall tower was left desolated due to the lack of funds. In the meantime, Italian inventor, Marconi successfully sent the wireless signal from England to Newfoundland. The Italian was named the inventor of the radio and became rich. The failure of Wardenclyffe was a major setback for Tesla, as he saw all his dreams crumbling right in front of his eyes. This led to his major nervous breakdown.

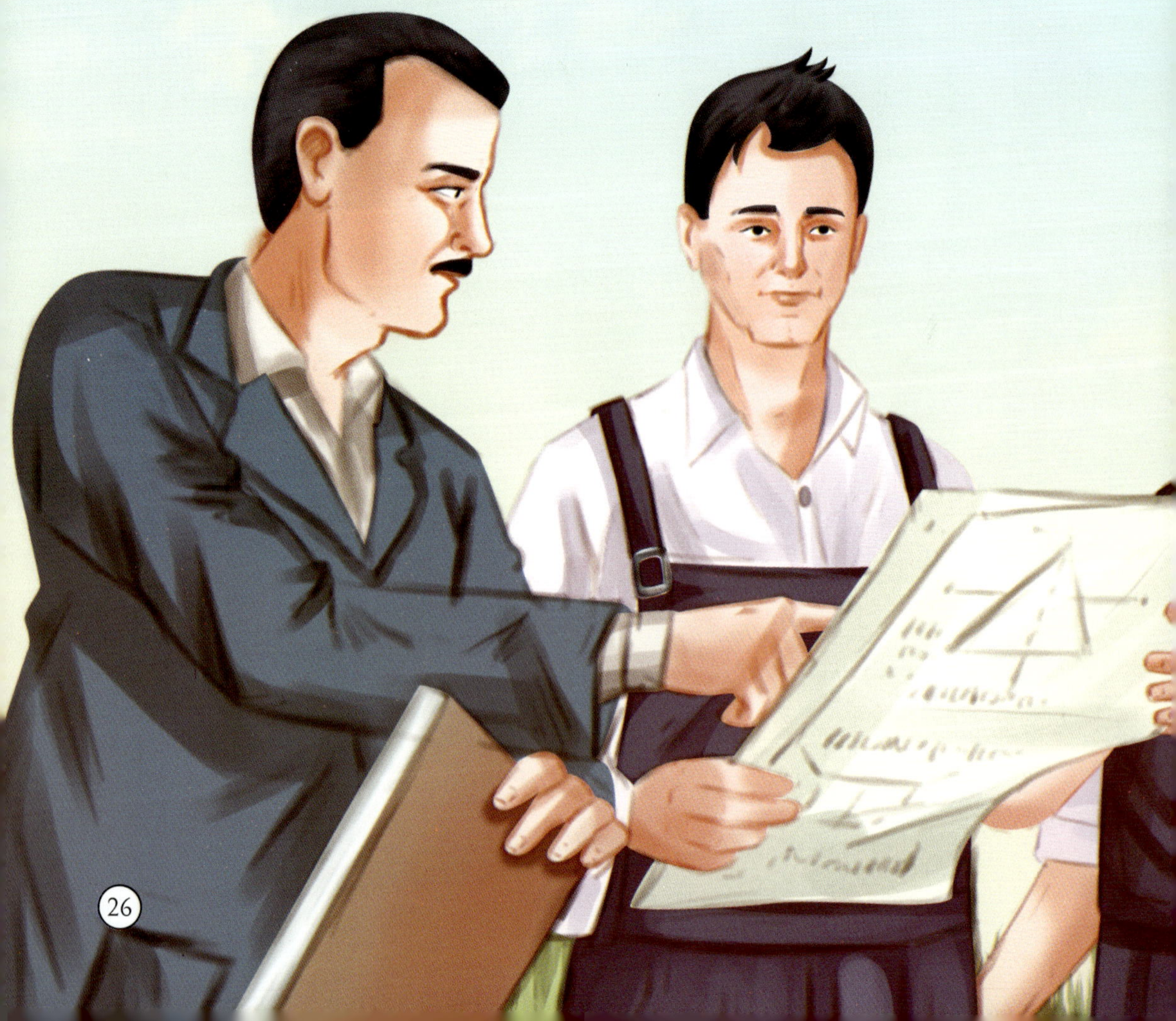

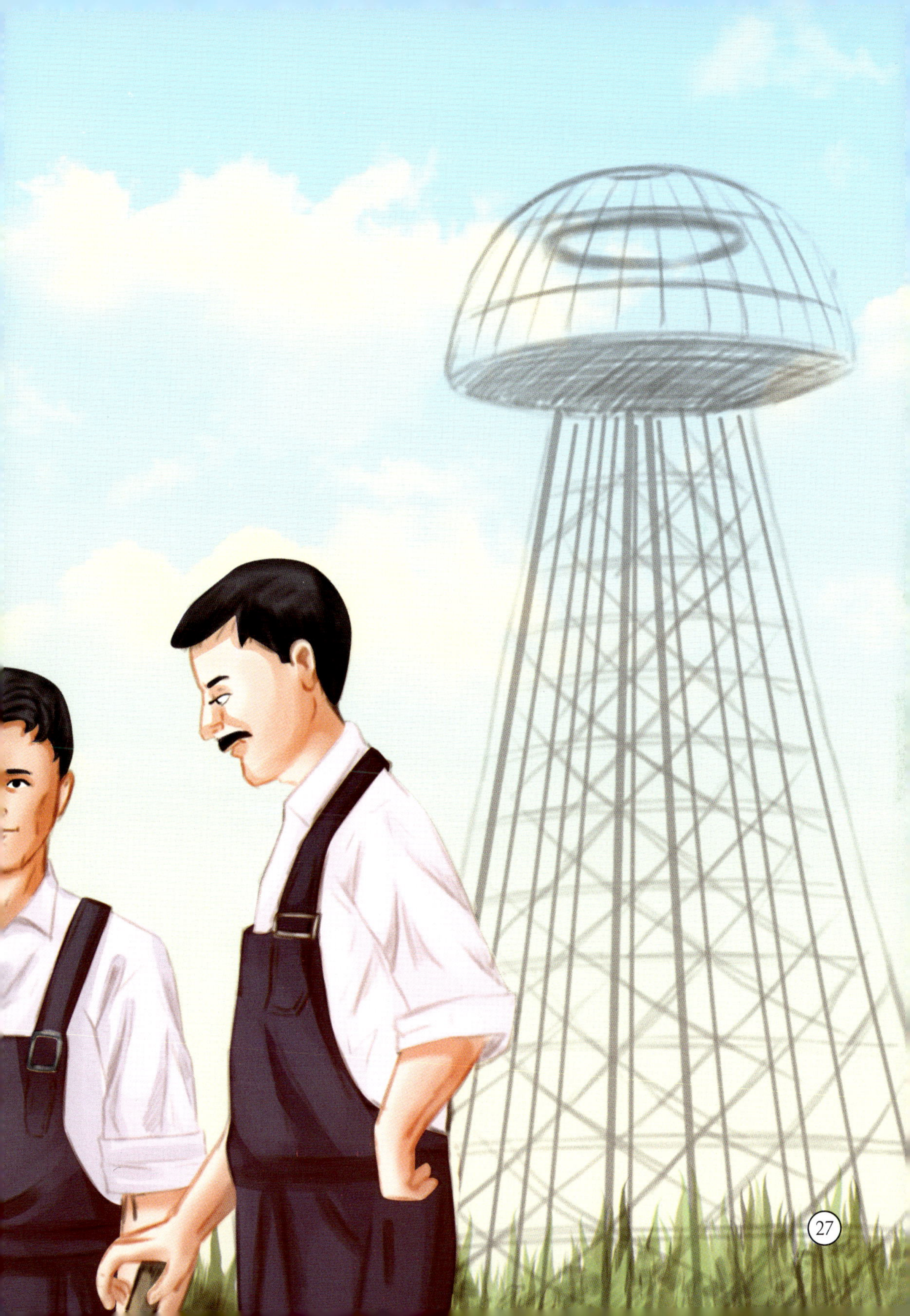

FROM STRUGGLES TO SOLACE

Around 1912, Tesla began to withdraw from the world. The failure of the Wardenclyffe Tower project had a huge impact on his psyche. He started showing signs of obsessive-compulsive disorder and was obsessed with cleanliness. He developed an abnormal sensitivity to sound and showed signs of erratic behavior. In his later years, he sought the company of birds and spent most of his time in nursing and feeding them.

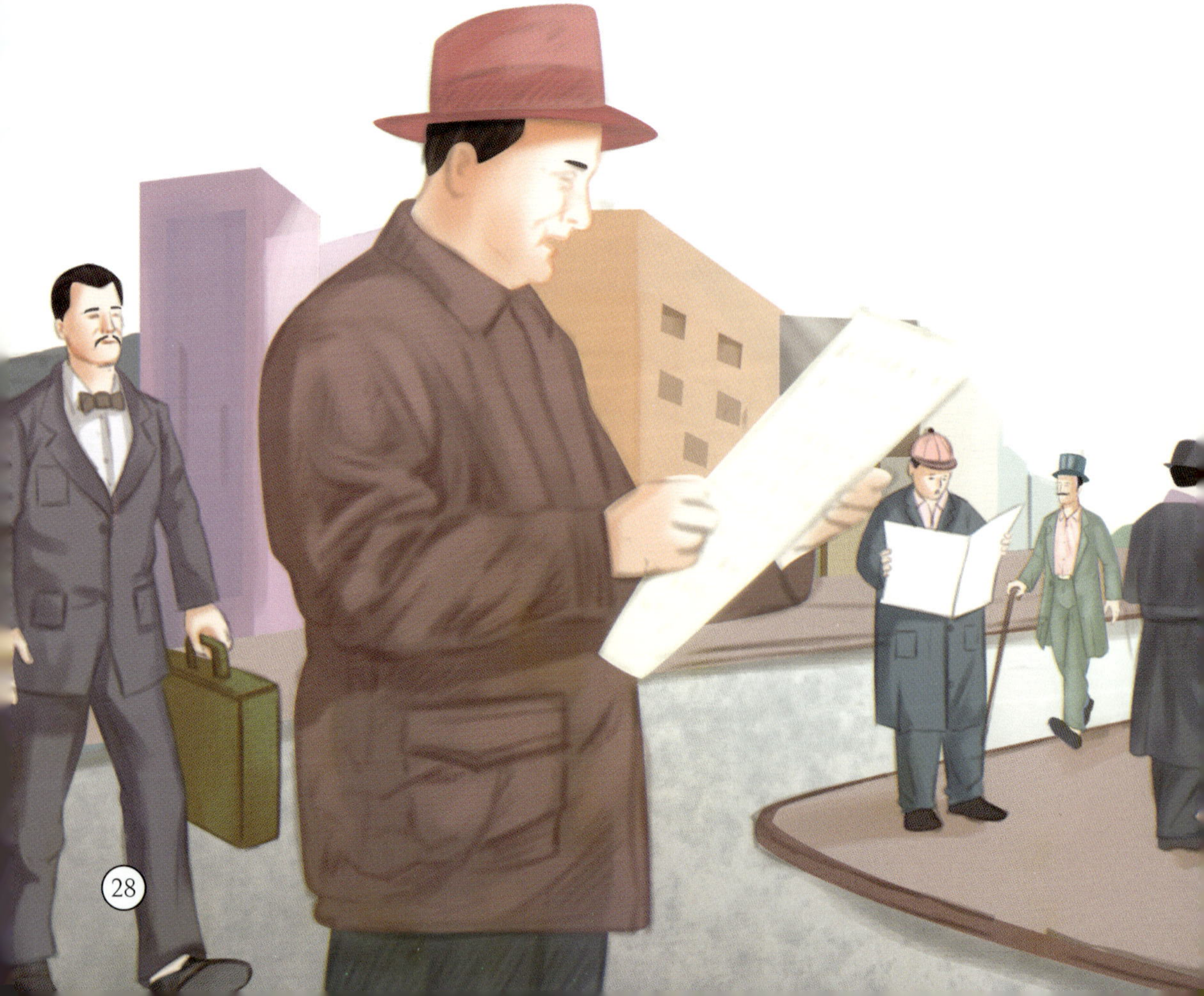

He met with an accident in 1937, that injured him gravely but still, he refrained from seeking any medical help. He never recovered completely after that. On 7 January 1943, Tesla was found dead in his hotel room.

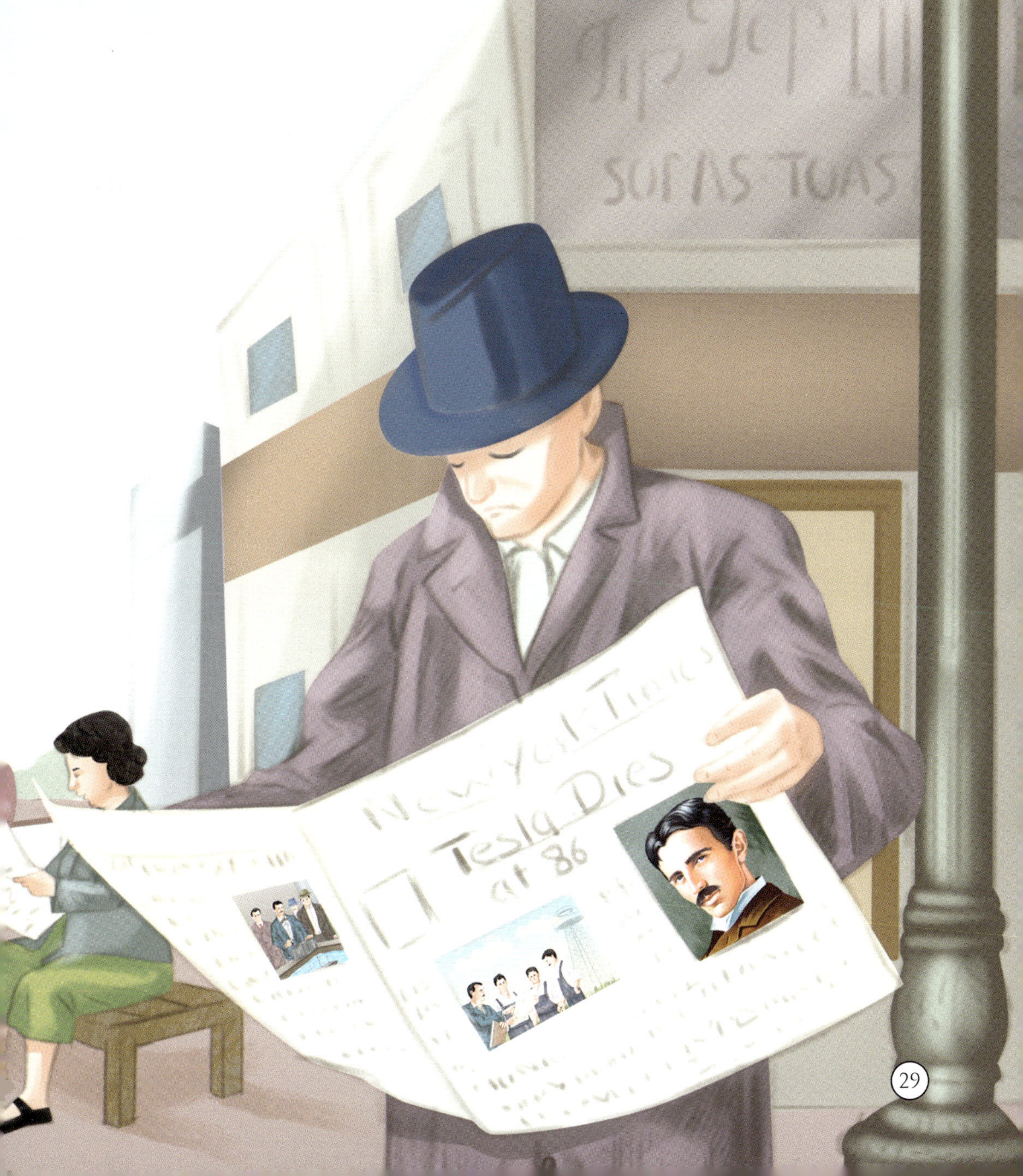
New York Times
Tesla Dies
at 86

SOME MEN DO BECOME IMMORTAL

It is difficult for words to do justice to Tesla's inventive mind and progressive ideas. He gave wings to the idea of alternating current (AC) and brought brightness to other people's life. He aimed to do better for the mankind. All his inventions have served to make the world a better place.

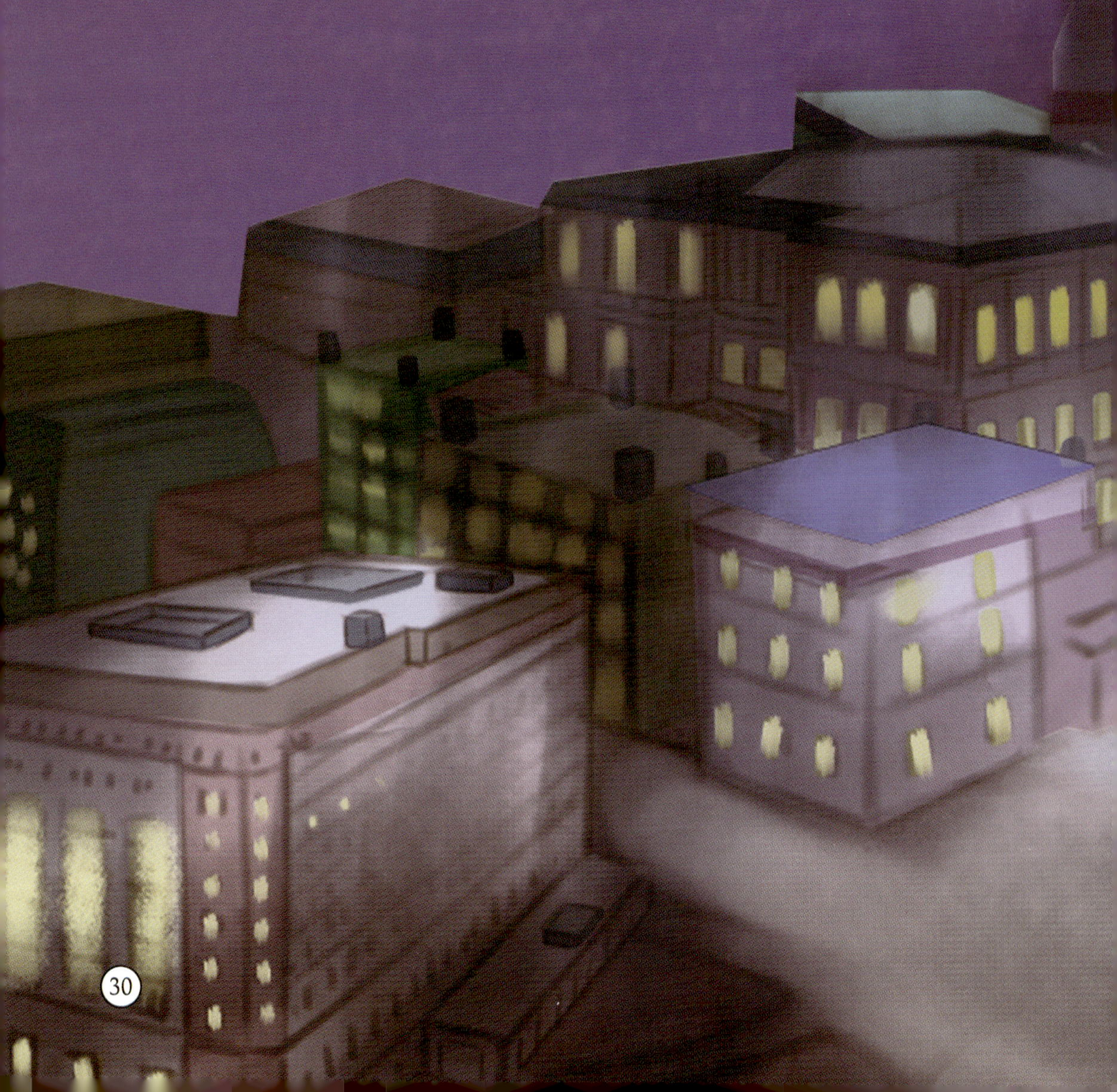

He met with an accident in 1937, that injured him gravely but still, he refrained from seeking any medical help. He never recovered completely after that. On 7 January 1943, Tesla was found dead in his hotel room.

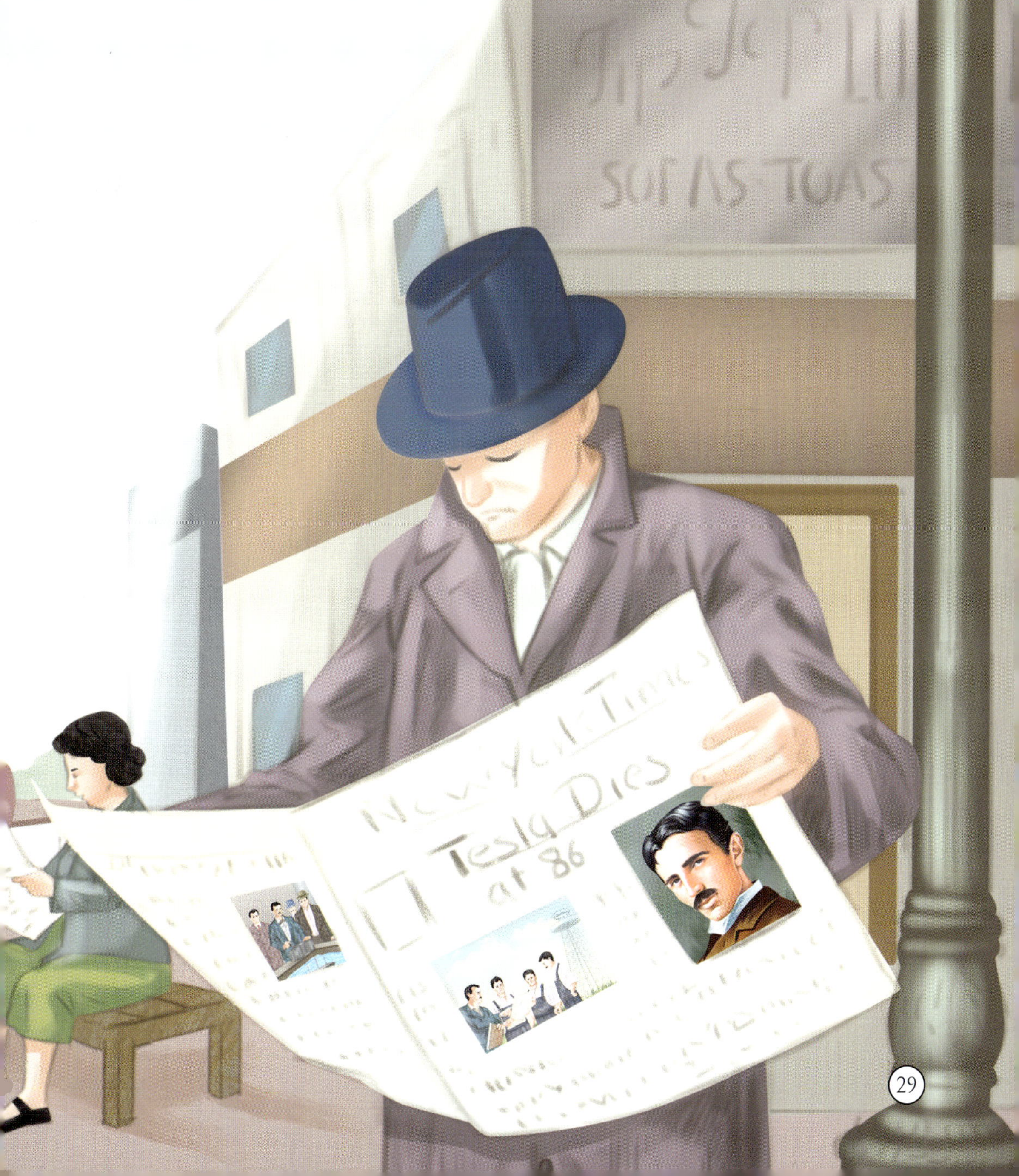
Tesla Dies
at 86

SOME MEN DO BECOME IMMORTAL

It is difficult for words to do justice to Tesla's inventive mind and progressive ideas. He gave wings to the idea of alternating current (AC) and brought brightness to other people's life. He aimed to do better for the mankind. All his inventions have served to make the world a better place.

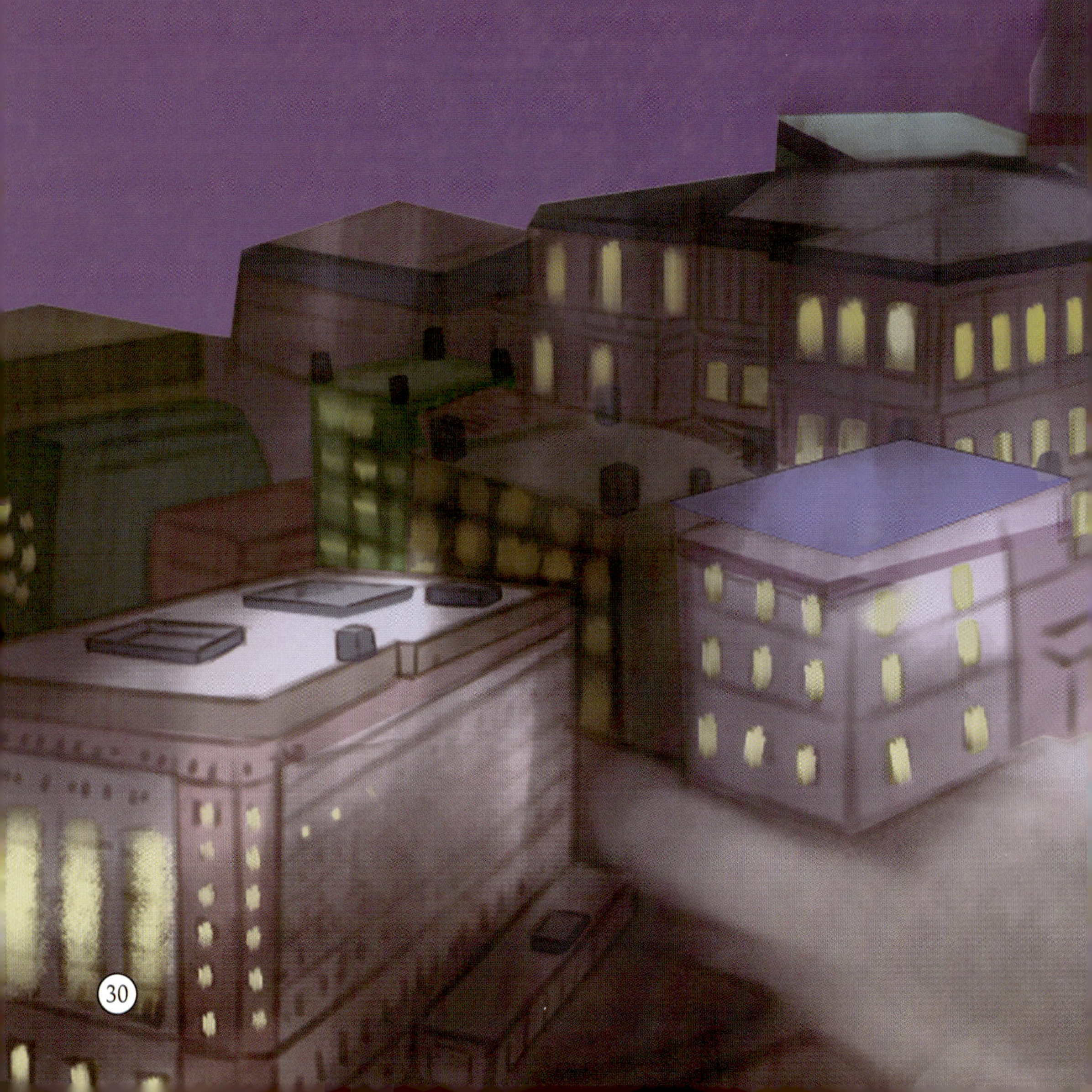

His credit was long due, ironically he received that credit and recognition for his work after his death. Tesla's name has become immortal, and he is an inspiration for several young inventors and engineers.

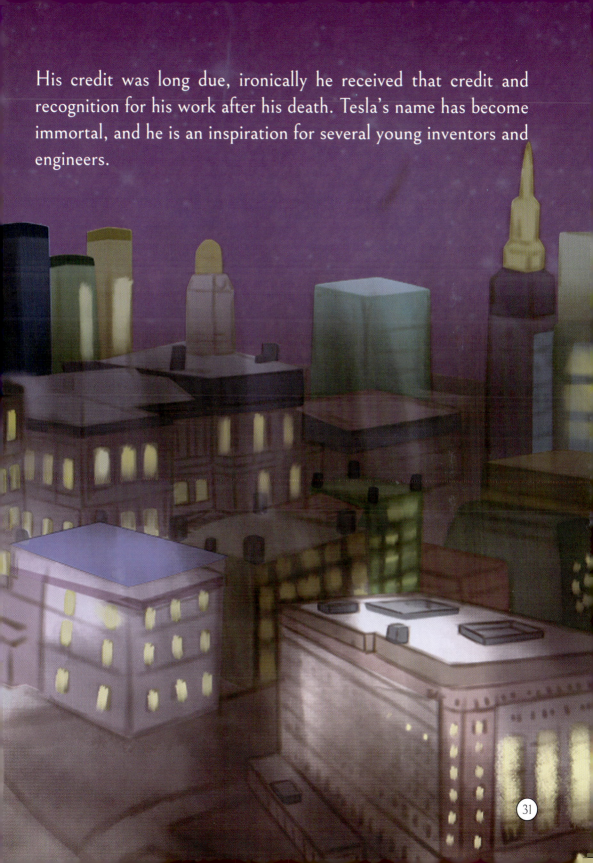

1856 : Nikola Tesla is born

1875 : Tesla Enrolls at Austrian Polytechnic College

1882 : Works for Continental Edison Company (Paris, France)

1884 : Tesla moves to United States

1885 : Nikola Tesla quits working for Edison

1886 : Inception of Tesla Electric Light and Manufacturing

1887 : Builds first AC induction motor;
War of Current begins

1891 : Tesla patents Tesla Coil

1898 : Tesla demonstrates wireless control

1901 : Construction of Wardenclyffe Tower begins

1943 : Tesla dies